The Singer's Series

Women's Edition

Standard Ballads

10 Great Songs in New Arrangements in Carefully Chosen Keys Especially for Singers

Arranged by Richard Walters

Contents

Performers on the CD:
Shannon Forsell, singer • Jim Connerly, Rick Walters, piano
Ken Gotschall, bass • Larry Sauer, drums

The piano accompaniments here present the spirit of the recorded trio accompaniments. Because the nature of this style of playing is improvisatory, they needn't be taken literally. This style of popular music asks a singer to do a bit with the vocal line, beyond the straight melody. The singers on the recording have deliberately presented their parts in a fairly conservative manner to aid you in learning the songs. You will certainly find other approaches in singing these songs, adding your own optional notes and phrasing.

ISBN 0-7935-8348-9

HAL•LEONARD®
CORPORATION
7777 W. BLUEMOUND RD. P.O. BOX 13819 MILWAUKEE, WI 53213

Visit Hal Leonard Online at
www.halleonard.com

ALL THE THINGS YOU ARE

Lyrics by OSCAR HAMMERSTEIN II
Music by JEROME KERN

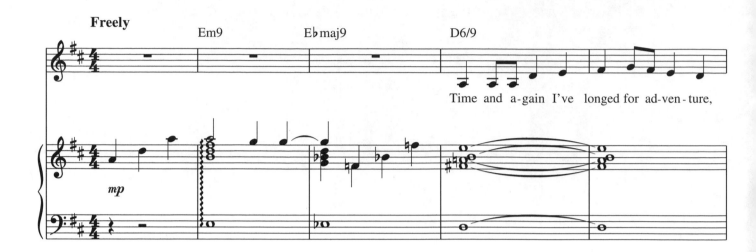

Time and a-gain I've longed for ad-ven-ture,

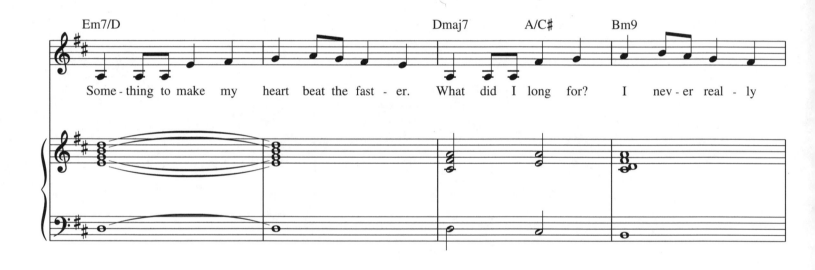

Some-thing to make my heart beat the fast-er. What did I long for? I nev-er real-ly knew.

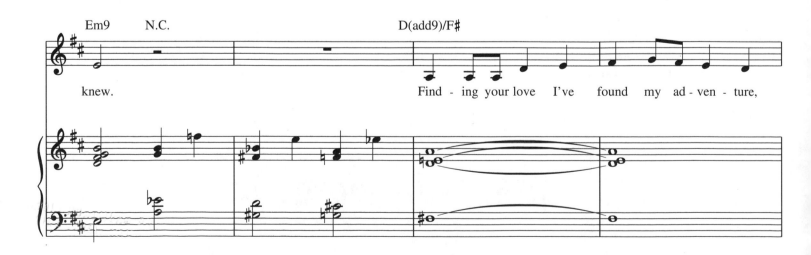

Find-ing your love I've found my ad-ven-ture,

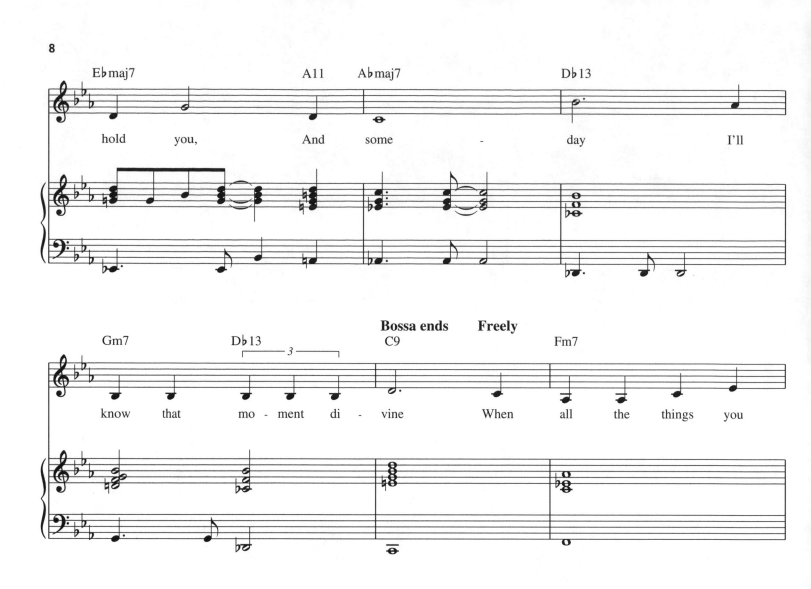

hold you, And some - day I'll

know that mo - ment di - vine When all the things you

Bossa ends **Freely**

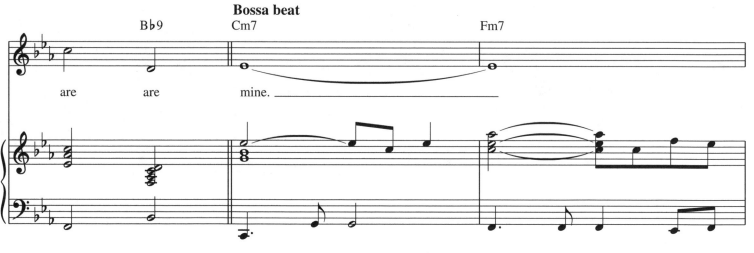

Bossa beat

are are mine. _____

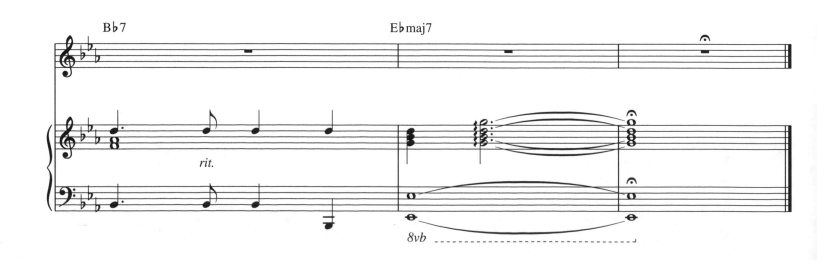

rit.

8vb

CALL ME IRRESPONSIBLE

Words by SAMMY CAHN
Music by JAMES VAN HEUSEN

AUTUMN LEAVES
(Les Feuilles Mortes)

English Lyric by JOHNNY MERCER
French Lyric by JACQUES PREVERT
Music by JOSEPH KOSMA

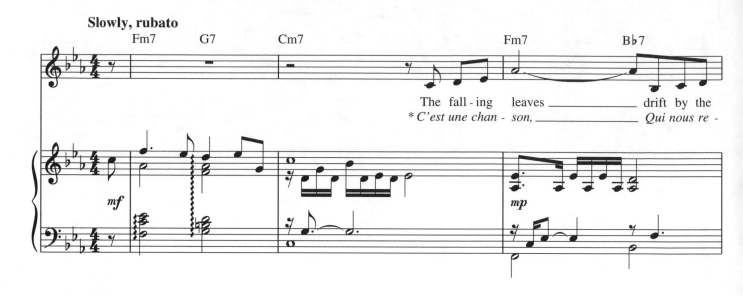

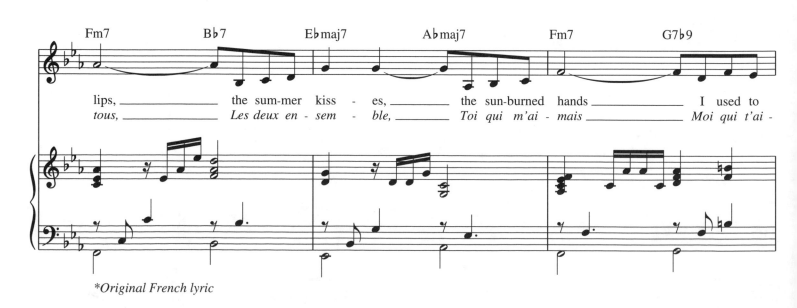

*Original French lyric

EAST OF THE SUN
(And West of the Moon)

Words and Music by
BROOKS BOWMAN

I'LL BE SEEING YOU

Lyric by IRVING KAHAL
Music by SAMMY FAIN

Ca - the - dral bells were toll - ing and our hearts sang

on, was it the spell of Par - is or the A - pril

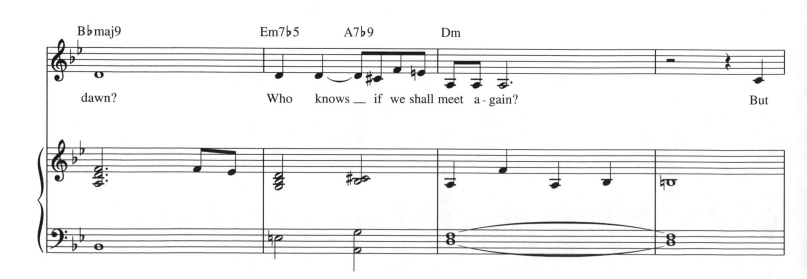

dawn? Who knows __ if we shall meet a - gain? But

26

I LEFT MY HEART IN SAN FRANCISCO

Words by DOUGLAS CROSS
Music by GEORGE CORY

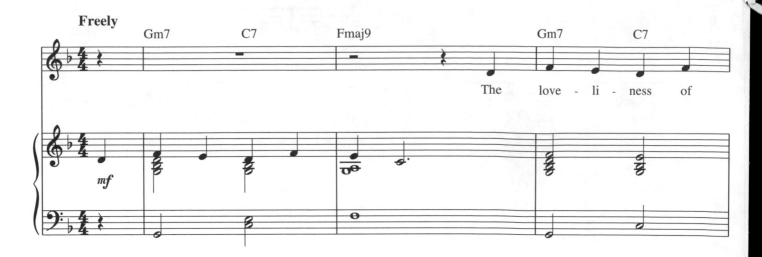

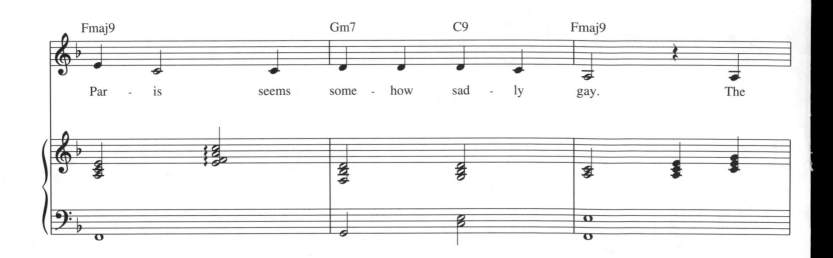

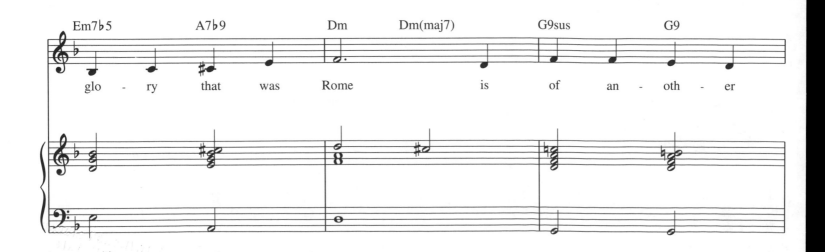

IN A SENTIMENTAL MOOD

Words and Music by DUKE ELLINGTON,
IRVING MILLS and MANNY KURTZ

ISN'T IT ROMANTIC?

Words by LORENZ HART
Music by RICHARD RODGERS

THE VERY THOUGHT OF YOU

Words and Music by
RAY NOBLE

THE WAY YOU LOOK TONIGHT

Words by DOROTHY FIELDS
Music by JEROME KERN

warm   And   your   cheeks   so   soft,

There   is   noth - ing   for   me   but   to   love   you

Just   the   way   you   look   to -

night. _____

ALL THE THINGS YOU ARE

Lyrics by OSCAR HAMMERSTEIN II
Music by JEROME KERN

CALL ME IRRESPONSIBLE

Words by SAMMY CAHN
Music by JAMES VAN HEUSEN

AUTUMN LEAVES
(Les Feuilles Mortes)

English Lyric by JOHNNY MERCER
French Lyric by JACQUES PREVERT
Music by JOSEPH KOSMA

Slowly, rubato

The fall-ing leaves ____ drift by the
C'est une chan - son, _____ Qui nous re -

win - dow, ___ the au-tumn leaves _____ of red and gold. I see your
sem - ble, ____ Toi tu m'ai - mais _____ Et je t'ai - mais. Nous vi - vions

lips, _____ the sum - mer kiss - es, _____ the sun-burned hands _____ I used to
tous, _____ Les deux en - sem - ble, _____ Toi qui m'ai - mais _____ Moi qui t'ai -

hold. Since you went a - way ____ the days grew long. ____ And soon I'll
mais. Mais la vie sé - pare ____ Ceux qui s'ai - ment ____ Tout dou - ce -

hear _____ old win - ter's song. But I miss you most of all, my
ment _____ Sans faire de bruit. Et la mer ef - fa - ce sur le

EAST OF THE SUN
(And West of the Moon)

Words and Music by
BROOKS BOWMAN

I'LL BE SEEING YOU

Words by IRVING KAHAL
Music by SAMMY FAIN

I LEFT MY HEART IN SAN FRANCISCO

Words by DOUGLAS CROSS
Music by GEORGE CORY

IN A SENTIMENTAL MOOD

Words and Music by DUKE ELLINGTON,
IRVING MILLS AND MANNY KURTZ

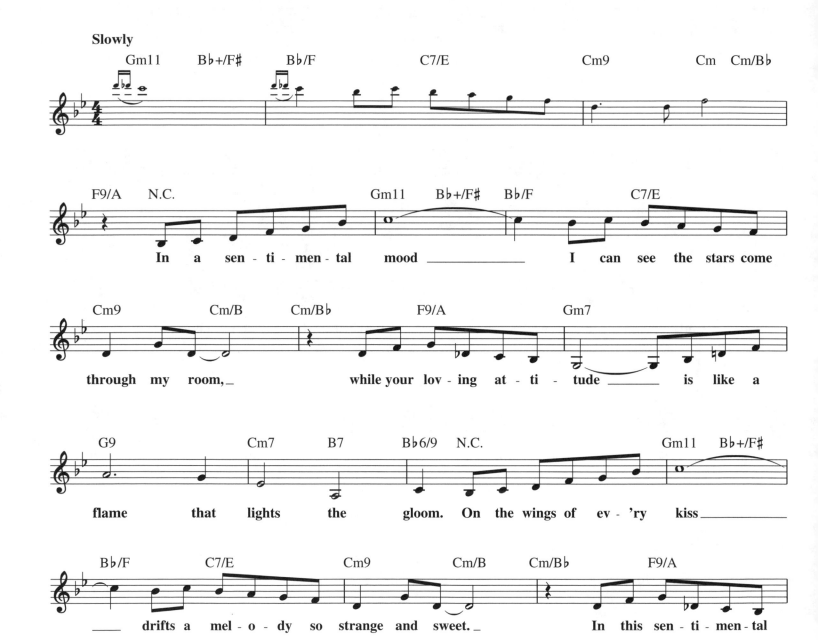

ISN'T IT ROMANTIC?

Words by LORENZ HART
Music by RICHARD RODGERS

THE VERY THOUGHT OF YOU

Words and Music by
RAY NOBLE

THE WAY YOU LOOK TONIGHT

Words by DOROTHY FIELDS
Music by JEROME KERN